LOVEMAKING IS THE ANGEL OF THE WATER

by

O.G.Doad

"SOMETIMES THERE

JUST ISN'T ENOUGH

VOMIT

IN THE WORLD."

— **STEPHEN FRY**

I opened the existence with a smirk

before our eyes, the body slipped

stay with me when bodies b-come st-icky

I fell asleep out of the material

lovemaking is the angel of the water

the sun fell for the ends

hatred flourishes after it's been hat-shed

torching

most violent axon

my tongue wades in her

oxidized eyes

the halo built under her arm

y

should unorthodox me be in control of my memory?

shiny interlocking

        swanecks

    pure symbal

enchantment, the poison,

treatment for skin diseases

I am smiling

I do not know if the door leaves or not

out of the picture we see

deus ex machina

I leave again

vomiting inside the sun

dopey sleepy imaginationality

the aura of a song met the minimum requirements

now be still my blargh

park bench is knocked up

black

music for your skin

a big fat odor

                fertile eye color

                                burning

he alerted the past

psychotic looming on-sight re-hanging

lovemaking

        recalling something

                gray

t/reason

hypothalamic hard drive

my tongue through it

dreams, music, fiery moon

blades of the wilderness

Whoop!

a fierce fiery beauty

s/he felt the mo(v)ment

I turned the lights up

I walked over the eyes

my thoughts

breaking away

scream

       the sweat bursts

              heroism

the day swinging my thoughts

the birds reared with a smile

the women in the bark trousers

my rerun

rainbow

killing him

the girl in the water

a heart

of my brain

erect-US

mud cadaver

must have been

lying in the

fluorescent tsunami

put those scissors away

dead flesh becomes clear

fiery moral tears

darkness is

mother nature

thinking

corner of mouth wants sanctions

ears are leaking their reasons

soul flow from the dust

the soul requires an abomination

I wake up amidst your body

people are glass fragments

the head decorated with the birds

soul is the dictionary

mind the crap

the child's burning

early years

the sand

the animal will rip

the urban fluorescent

hypothalamus

in peaces

wickedness breathes sticky sweat

the girl

even more sticky sweat

B(I)T

of a

B(®)AT

your body was discovered by my fingers

as violent as the apple pie

I am a soft, fuzzy little party

batter closer to my heart

the walls

for years

they were

my heart

back on those days

whenever I could

I tried to find more

smell

the rage

sings

the body

the stimulant

a box of wine

images of terror

the man

smell

I am obscene shiny new brand

it is the spring

I saw the death

with hand brake on

complex with the skin

only the lonely

        the heartache's

                all grown up

eat your toenail

irrigate the eccentric individuals

the bridges built by the sewers

saw my eyes to the music

I do not glow

individuals

look at my hand

the gray

the darkness

my nose bleeds

put your hand inside the slight madness

we are extremely large

and

pitch-black

and

I will eat your woman

I walked into the bedroom with a lighter

burning outside of the time

a heart for you to breathe

perhaps

we now can open the existence

with a smirk

happy, wavy freshness

step over the moral threshold

I'm getting myself

immensely

watch the forefinger

at the next green lights

bats hanging from the eye

I would kick your attitude

I lay in the sleeping bags of the shame

shame

blame

game

became

tame

lame

Tr

end.

www.ingramcontent.com/pod-product-compliance
Lightning Source LLC
Chambersburg PA
CBHW060132050426
42448CB00010B/2081